The ABRSM

SINGING FOR

MUSICAL THEATRE

Songbook

Grade 4

This is a selection of the songs from the ABRSM Singing for Musical Theatre syllabus. For the complete repertoire lists and full details of exam requirements, please see the current syllabus at www.abrsm.org/sfmt. Musical theatre is a vibrant and energetic contemporary art form, and with songs exploring different characters and styles of music there should be something for everyone, whether you are preparing for an exam, audition, or the stage, or just because you love singing songs from shows!

ABRSM would like to thank Rachel Lyske for her invaluable advice.

First published in 2020 by Hal Leonard Europe Limited and ABRSM (Publishing) Ltd, a wholly owned subsidiary of ABRSM.

Exclusively distributed worldwide by Hal Leonard Europe Limited

ISBN 978 1 83992 004 2
AB 3997

Music Origination by John Rogers — Top Score Music
Printed on materials from sustainable sources

ABRSM

Contact us:
Hal Leonard
7777 West Bluemound Road
Milwaukee, WI 53213
Email: info@halleonard.com

In Europe, contact:
Hal Leonard Europe Limited
42 Wigmore Street
Marylebone, London, W1U 2RY
Email: info@halleonardeurope.com

In Australia, contact:
Hal Leonard Australia Pty. Ltd.
4 Lentara Court
Cheltenham, Victoria, 3192 Australia
Email: info@halleonard.com.au

LULLABY OF BROADWAY

42nd Street

Words by Al Dubin (1891–1945)
Music by Harry Warren (1893–1981)

Come on a-long and lis-ten to____ the lull-a-by of Broad-way.

The hip - hoo-ray and bal-ly-hoo,____ the lull-a-by of Broad-way.
The hi - dee-hi and boop-a-doo,____ the lull-a-by of Broad-way.

Exam requirements: without repeat

4

AB 3997

sleep   tight,   let's call it a day.____ Hey!__

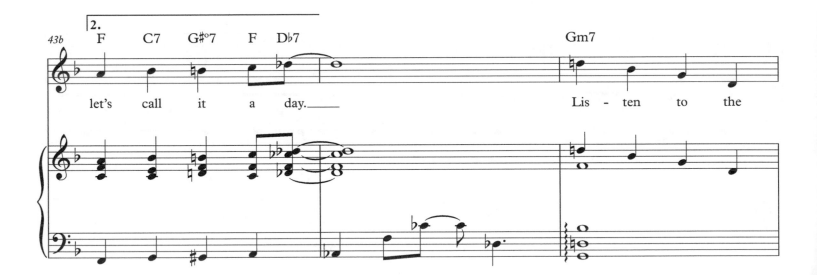

let's call it a day.____   Lis - ten to the

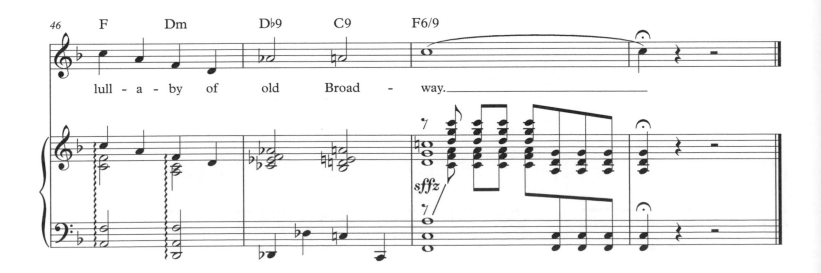

lull - a - by of old Broad - way._____

MATCHMAKER

Fiddler on the Roof

Words by Sheldon Harnick (born 1924)
Music by Jerry Bock (1928–2010)

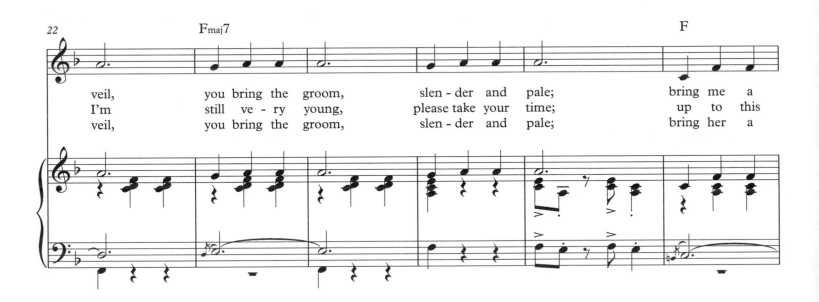

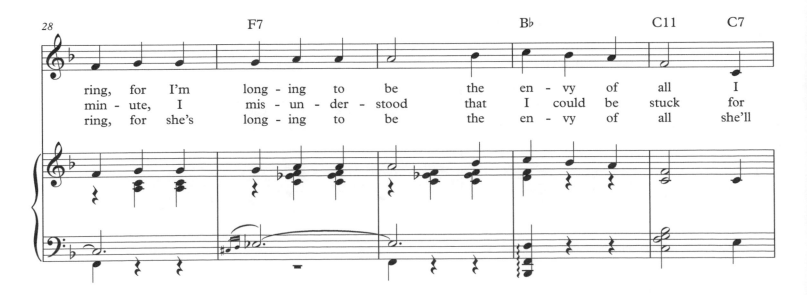

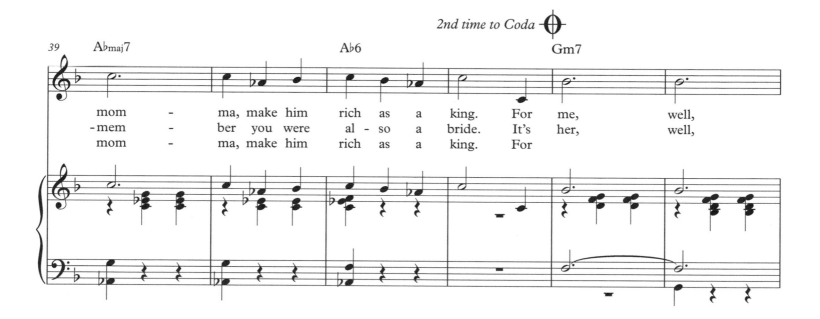

YOU WERE MEANT FOR ME

Singin' in the Rain

Words by Arthur Freed (1894-1973)
Music by Nacio Herb Brown (1896-1964)

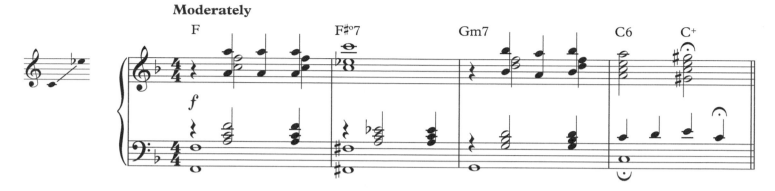

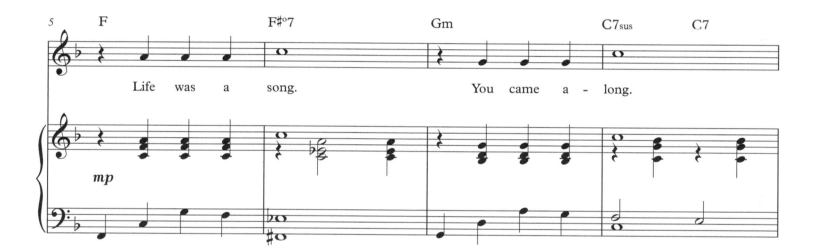

Life was a song. You came a - long.

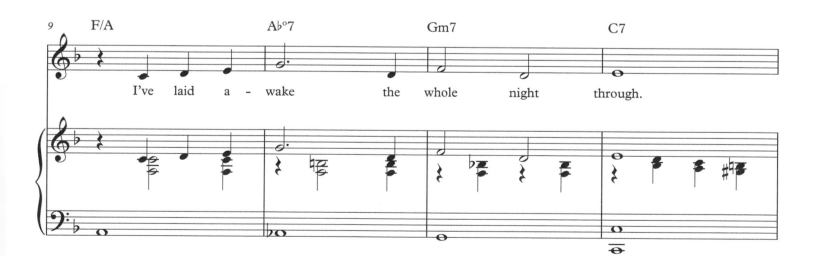

I've laid a - wake the whole night through.

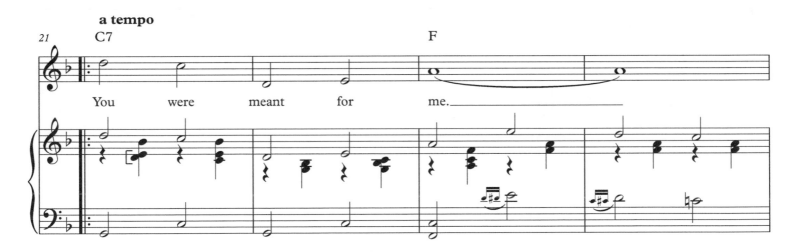

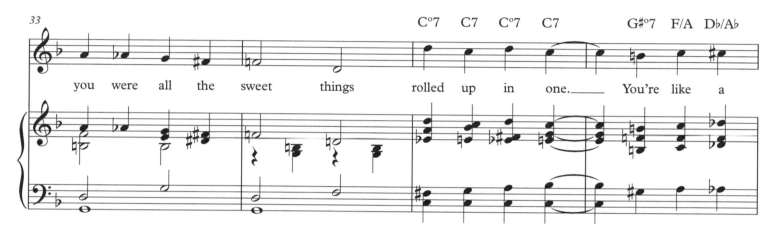

I'm con - tent the an - gels must have sent you and they

meant you just for me.

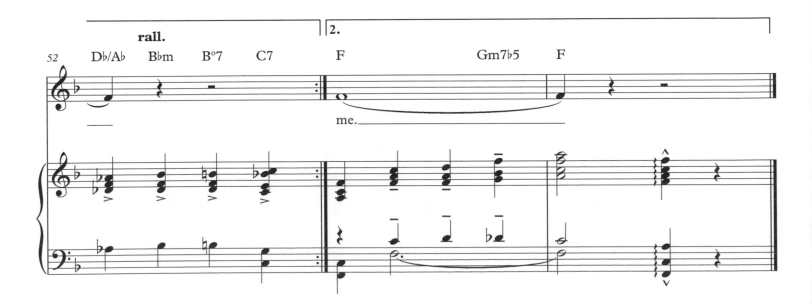

me.

PURE IMAGINATION

Willy Wonka and the Chocolate Factory

Words and music by
Leslie Bricusse (born 1931)
Anthony Newley (1931-99)

Exam requirements: straight to coda after b. 26

18

AB 3997

no life I know to com - pare with pure i - ma - gi - na - tion. Liv - ing

D.S. al Coda

there you'll be free if you tru - ly wish to be.

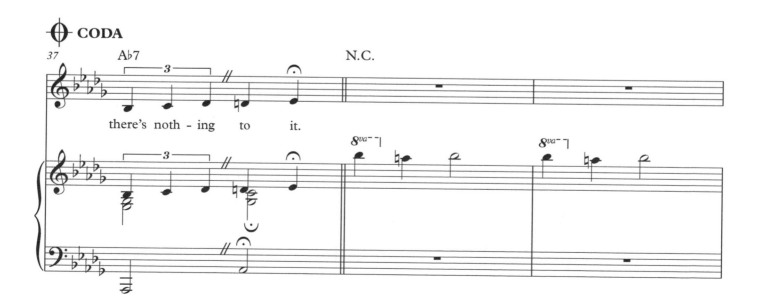

there's noth - ing to it.

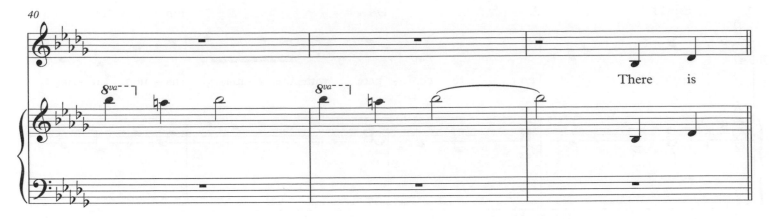

rubato

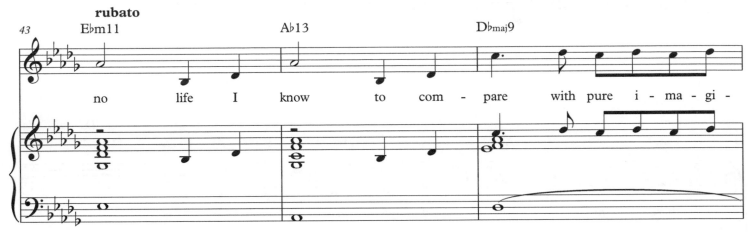

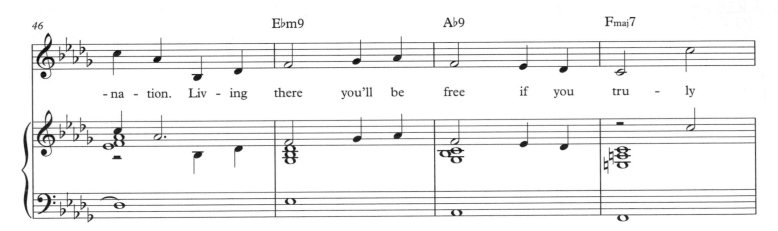

Repeat to fade

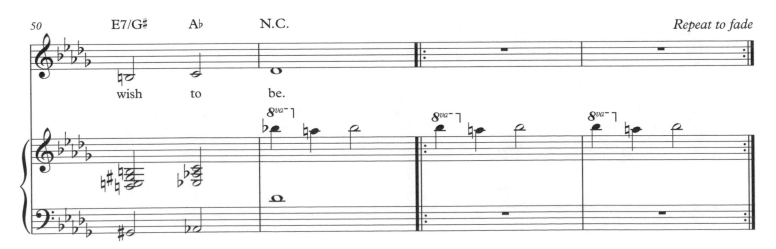

ELECTRICITY

Billy Elliot

Music by Elton John (born 1947)
Lyrics by Lee Hall (born 1966)

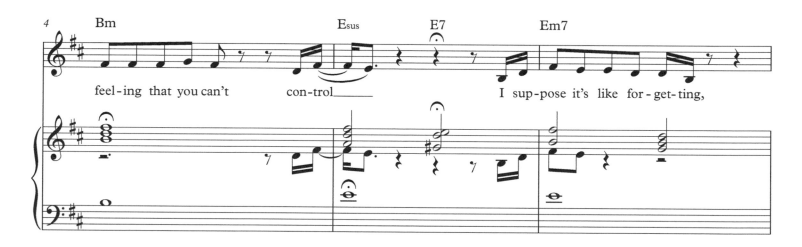

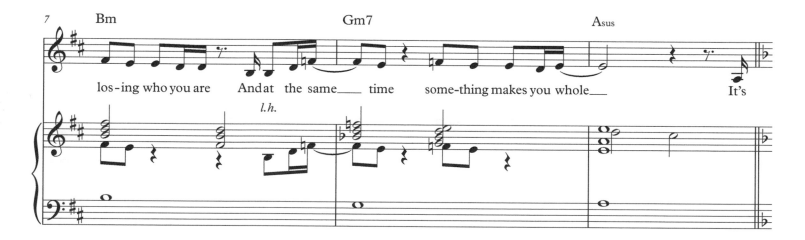

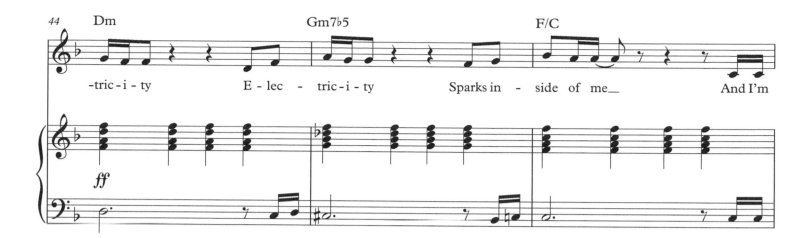

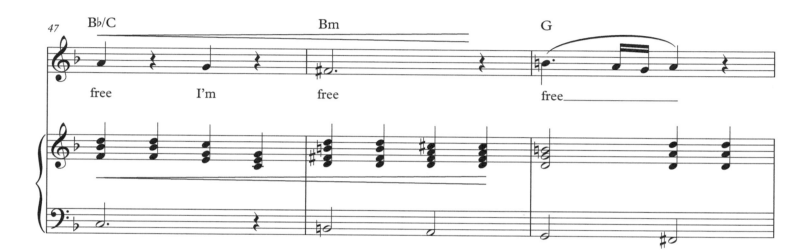

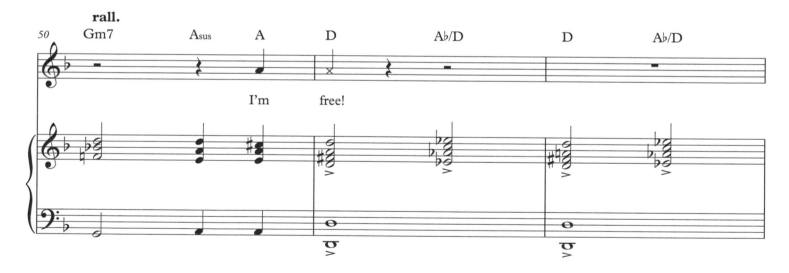

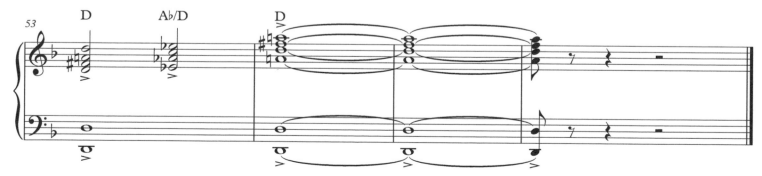

THE WORLD ABOVE

The Little Mermaid

Music by Alan Menken (born 1949)
Lyrics by Glenn Slater (born 1968)

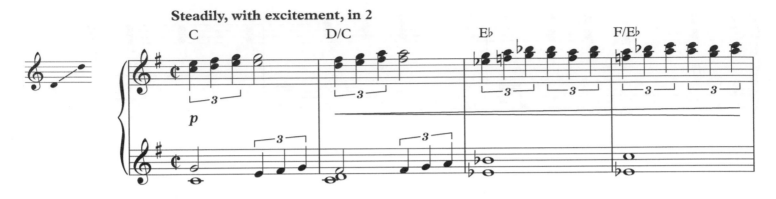

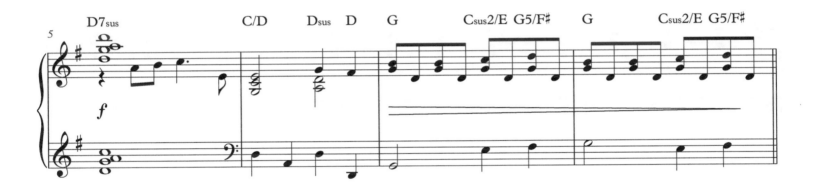

blue here. I feel com-plete-ly new here in the world a-

-bove. It's like my life was wrong.

And some-how now at last I'm in my own

skin, up here in the world a - -

-bove. There's so much light here,

light and space. The sun's so bright here up -

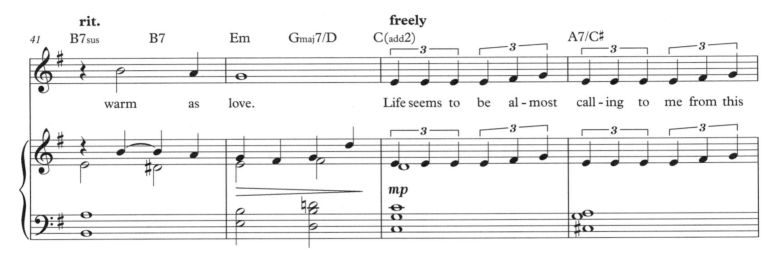

SISTER ACT

Sister Act

Words by Glenn Slater (born 1968)
Music by Alan Menken (born 1949)

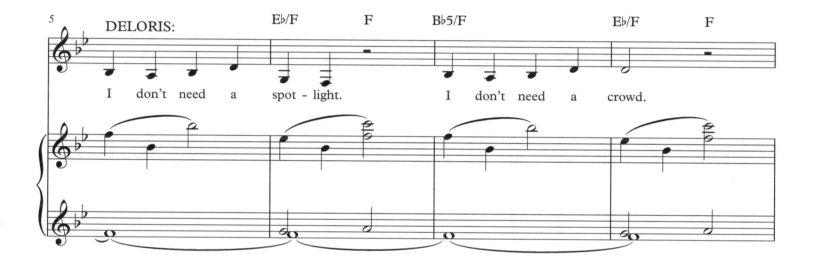

30
Ebadd9 F Bb Ebmaj7 F Gm
sis-ters, stand-ing strong, I'm on the stage where I be-long.
34
C9/E Ebmaj7 Bbmaj9/D C9(sus4) C9
And noth-ing's ev - er gon - na change that fact. I'm
39
Bb/F F Bb/F Ebmaj7/F F7 Bb F/Bb Bb E/F# F# E/F# F#
part of one ter - ri - fic sis - ter act. And,
Ped.
43
Badd9 B Emaj7/G# F#/A# Badd9 B Emaj7/G# F#/A#
yes, I love that spot-light. Yes, I crave ac - claim.
mf

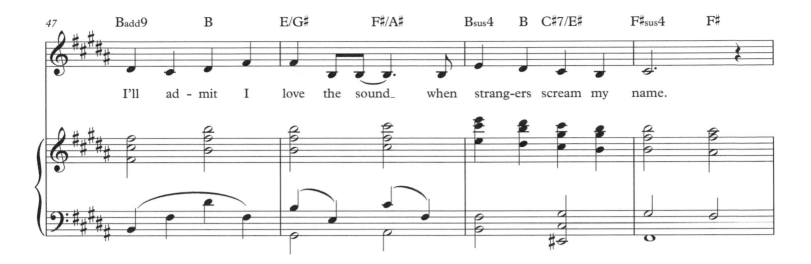

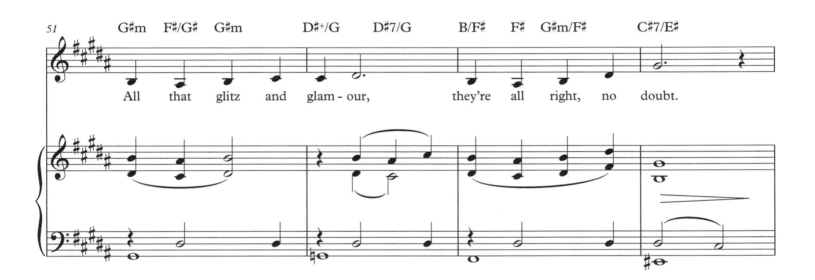

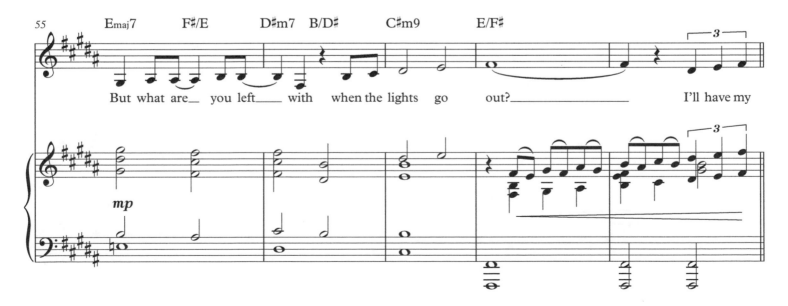

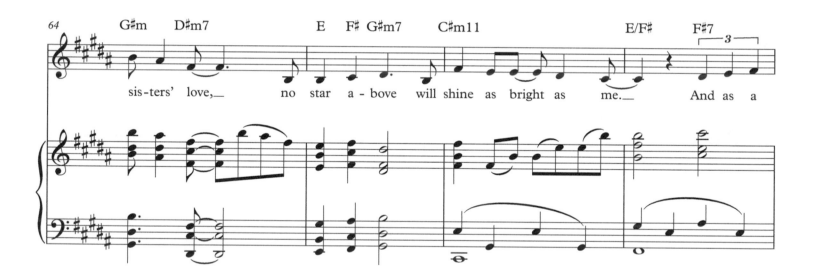

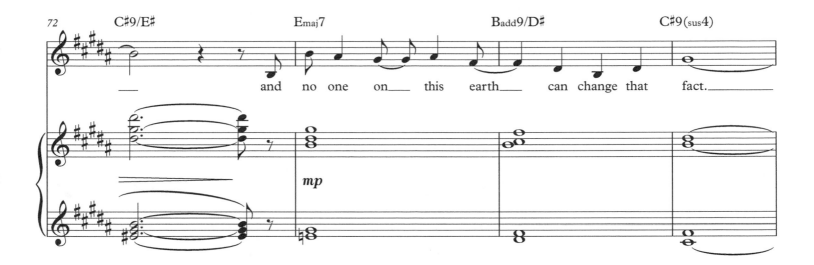

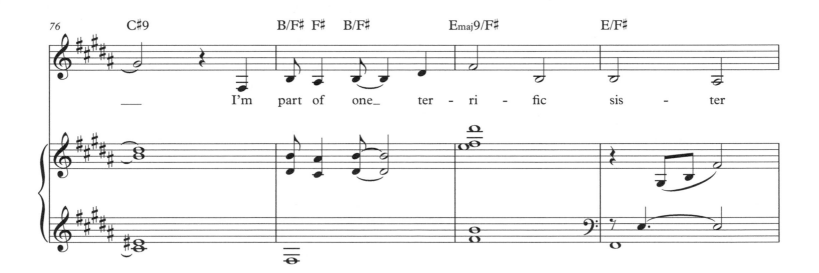

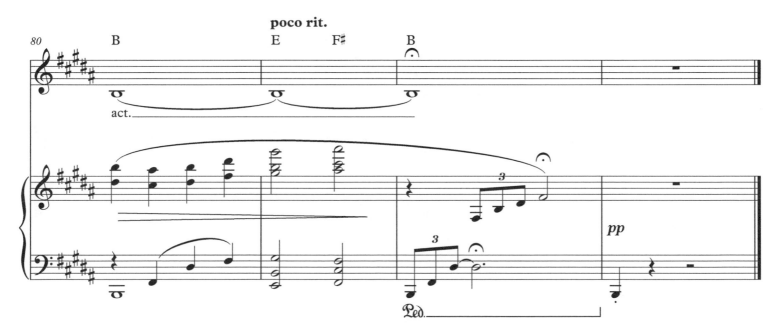

I'M NOT SAYING A WORD

Blood Brothers

Words and music by
Willy Russell (born 1947)

Moderately

EDWARD:

1. If

A   F#m7   D   E   A   E/G#   F#m7

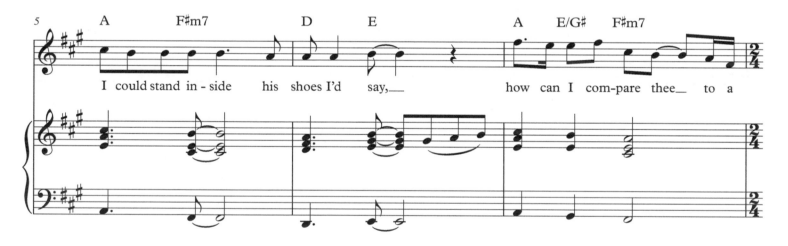

I could stand in - side his shoes I'd say,___ how can I com-pare thee___ to a

D   E   A   Fm7   D   E

sum-mer's day.___ I'd take a page in all the pa-pers,_ I'd an-nounce it on the news if

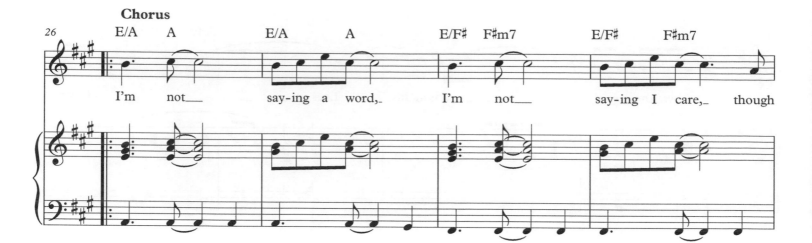

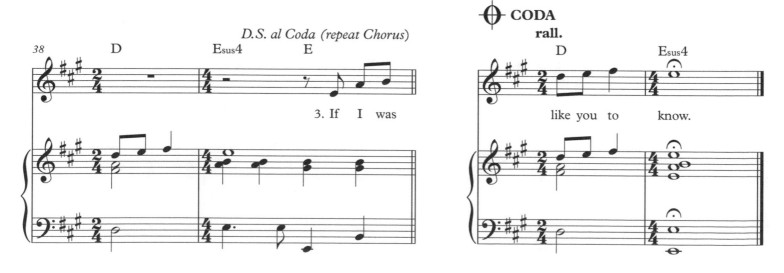

EASY STREET

Annie

Lyric by Martin Charnin (1934–2019)
Music by Charles Strouse (born 1928)

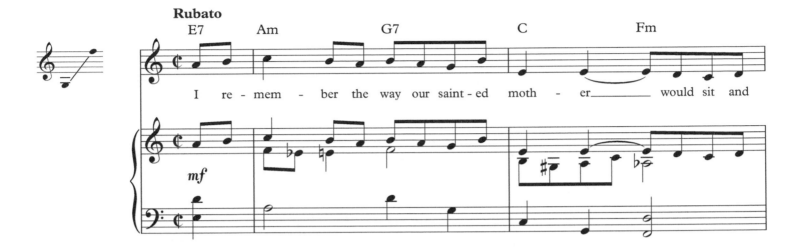

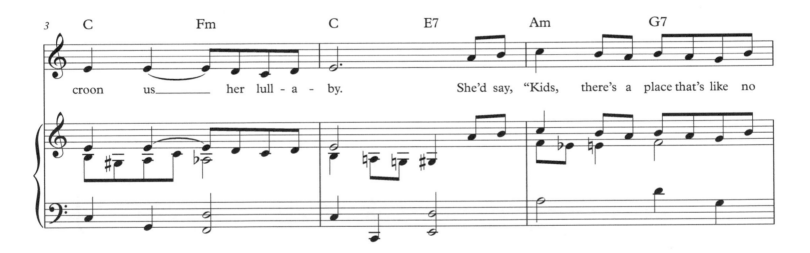

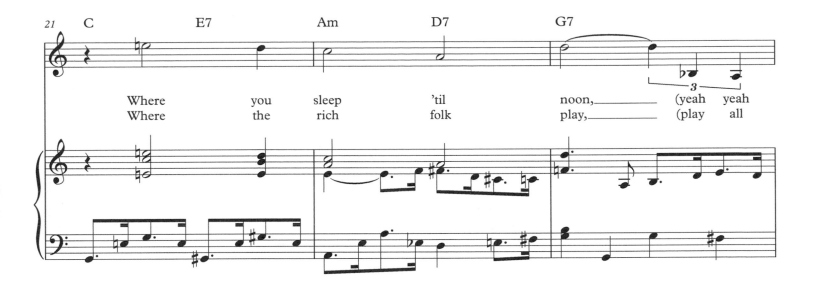

Where you sleep 'til noon,_____ (yeah yeah
Where the rich folk play,_____ (play all

yeah!)
day!)

She'd re - peat,
Move them feet,

"Eas - y Street,
Eas - y Street,

bet - ter
when_____ you

42

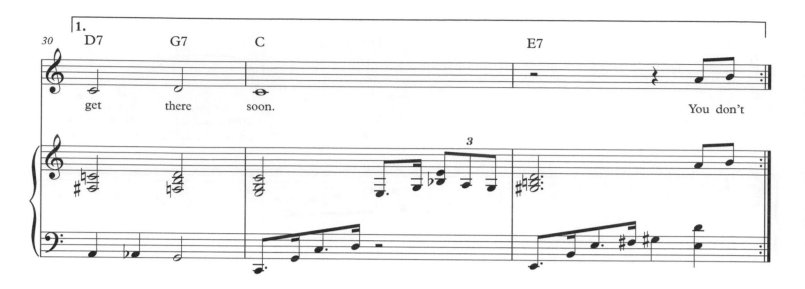

AB 3997

OUT THERE

Barnum

Music by Cy Coleman (1929-2004)
Lyrics by Michael Stewart (1924-87)

Staying home, living day by day may be safe but it can't be duller,
Turning back should the highway bend, turning down ev'ry chance you're given,

Seeing things only black and grey when the world is alive with colour.
Takes the risk out of life, but friend, how the hell can you call that livin'.

Once in his life ev-'ry man de-cides, Once when he stands where the road de-vides,

Once on a hill as the morn-ing grows, Once if he will he can see those

fires glow, flags stream - ing, spires

grow, tow'rs gleam - ing. In a land where the dawn is clear,

In a sky where the sun's for - ev - er, On a plain where it's spring all year,

And the dark of the night comes nev - er. Some - where, out there,

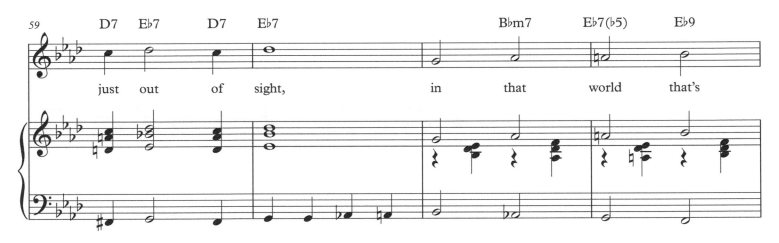

just out of sight, in that world that's

shin - ing with light Ain't each man a -

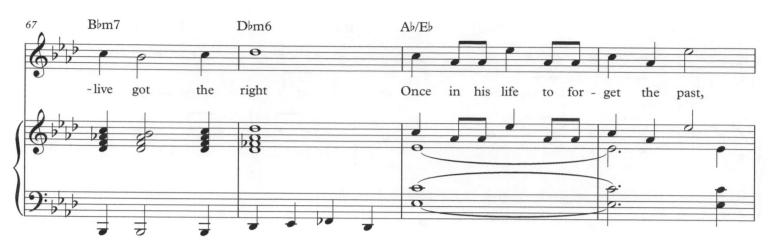

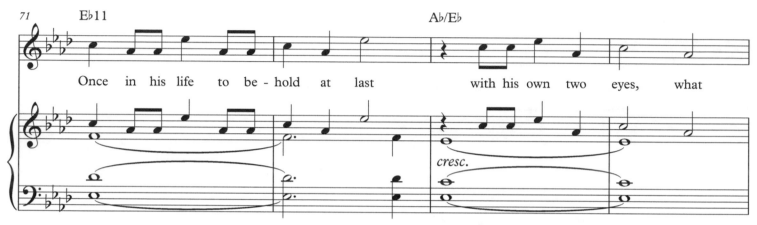

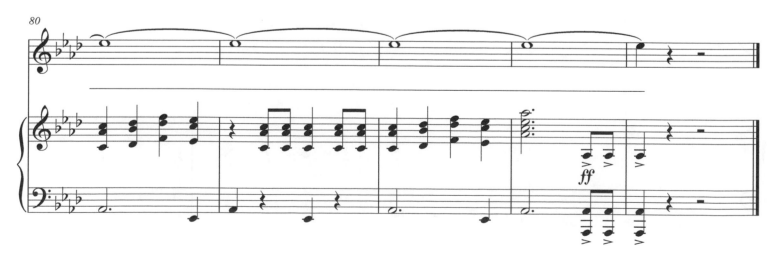

STEPSISTERS' LAMENT

Cinderella

Lyrics by Oscar Hammerstein II (1895-1960)
Music by Richard Rodgers (1902-79)

Why would a fel-low want a girl like her, a frail and fluf-fy beau-ty?

Why can't a fel-low ev-er once pre-fer a sol-id girl like me? She's a froth-y lit-tle

AB 3997

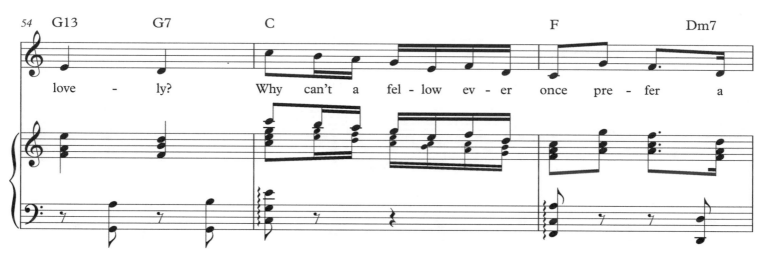

IF MY FRIENDS COULD SEE ME NOW

Sweet Charity

Music by Cy Coleman (1929-2004)
Lyrics by Dorothy Fields (1904-74)

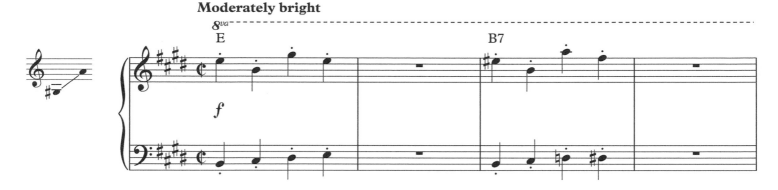

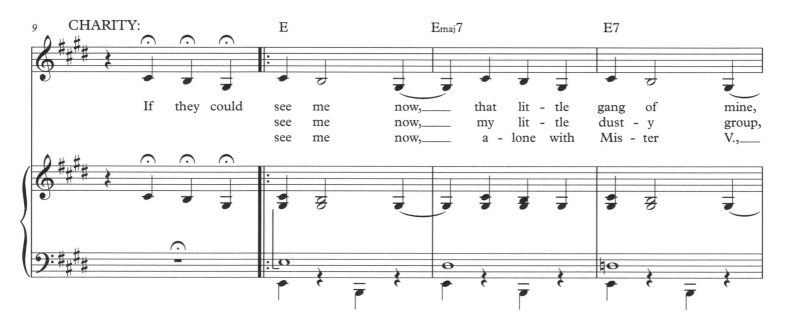

CHARITY:

If they could see me now, that lit - tle gang of mine,
see me now, my lit - tle dust - y group,
see me now, a - lone with Mis - ter V.,

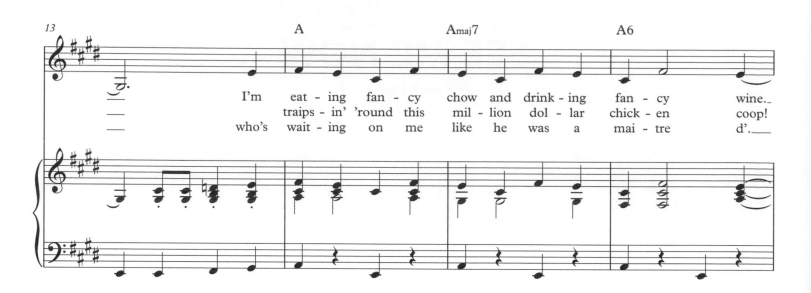

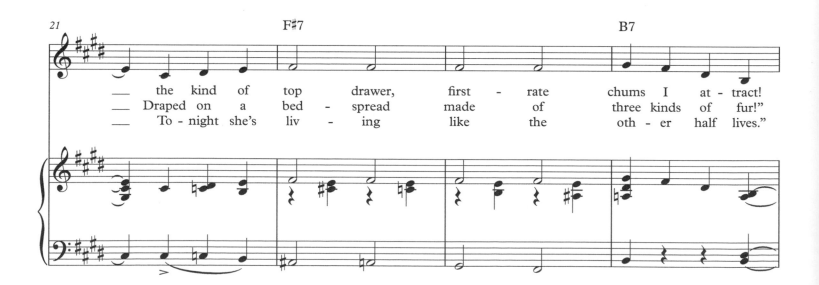

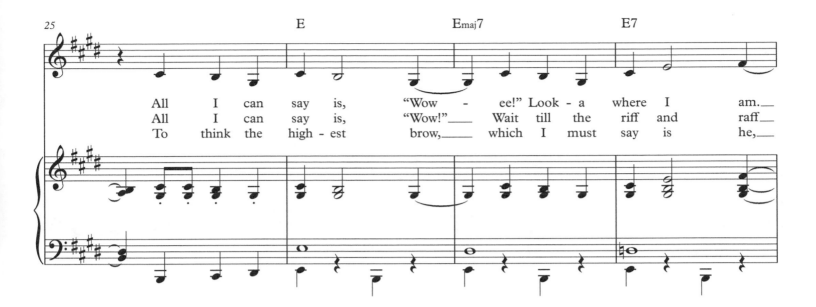

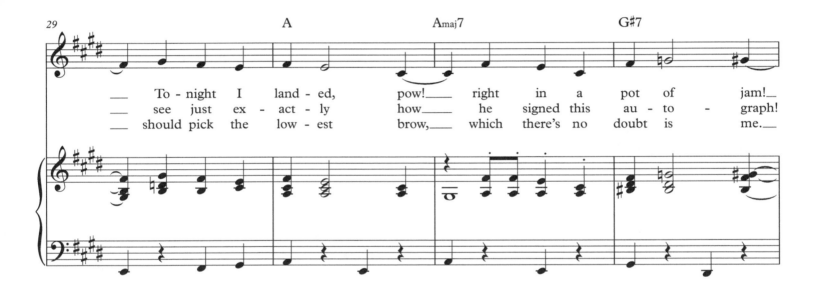

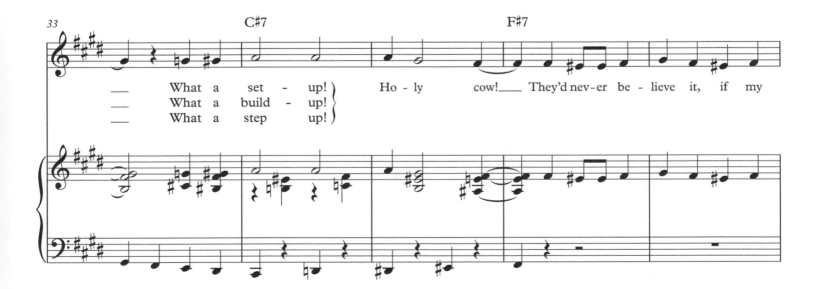